FEELINGS

Published by
CREATIVE EDUCATIONAL SOCIETY, INC.
Mankato, Minnesota 56001

Library of Congress Catalog Card No. 70-125915
ISBN 87191-045-4

Feelings

by Phoebe and Tris Dunn
words by Judy Dunn

to Molly and Emily

HOW DO YOU FEEL INSIDE?

How do you feel on Christmas morning? And how do you
feel after you've done something wrong? Certainly not
the same way. You feel different ways at different
times. Sometimes you feel so happy you want to shout.
Sometimes you feel sad inside. The different ways you
feel are called EMOTIONS. Most emotions are either
sad or happy, but there are different ways of feeling
sad and happy. You can feel very sad or just a little bit
sad. And you can feel very happy or just a little bit
happy. If you're sad, you frown or cry. And if you're
happy, you smile or laugh. Other people can tell how
you feel inside by what they see on your outside.
Let's look at some of your emotions and find out what
happens when you feel them . . .

ANGER

Probably the saddest way you ever felt was the angriest. Your mother called it a tantrum. Tantrums don't last too long because they wear you out. They're so awful you can't even talk. All you can do is yell.

CRYING

When you cry, you show it, you are unhappy. Emotions aren't things that you can touch or see, but you *can* touch and see your tears. Tears are warm and taste salty. When you cry like this you sob. Sobbing is noisy. Sometimes you keep on sobbing after you're through crying. You can't help it.

Some crying is quieter th[an] sobbing. Tears fill up your ey[es] and . . .

trickle down your cheeks, [but] you don't make much noi[se]. Sometimes your chin wiggl[es] too.

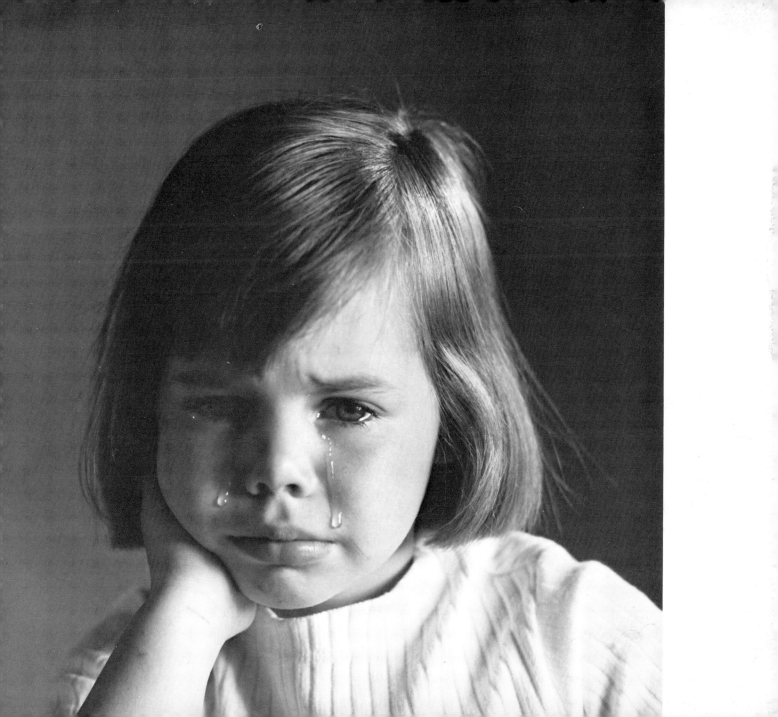

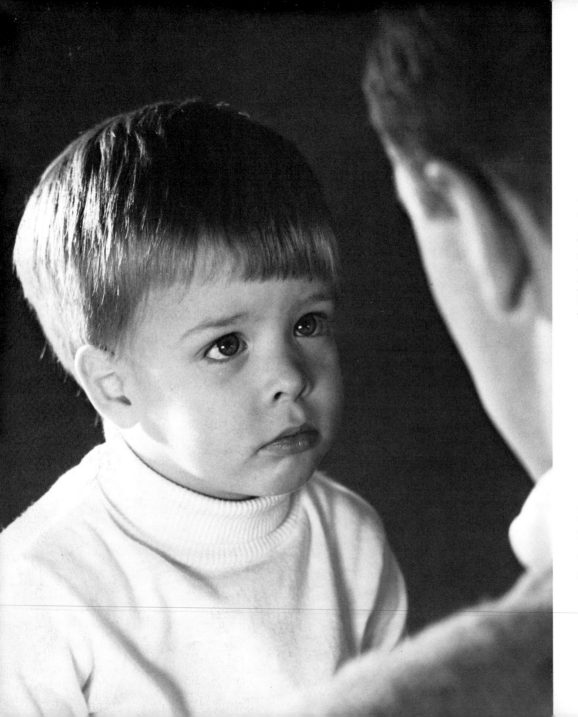

GUILT

After you've done someth[ing]
wrong, you feel guilty. It's [not]
a happy way of feeling. Som[e]
times your father talks serio[us]
ly with you when you've be[en]
bad. He helps you understa[nd]
what's right and what's wro[ng.]

Feeling guilty is an ins[ide]
feeling. Your outside usua[lly]
doesn't show it. You just th[ink]
about it a lot.

JEALOUSY

Feeling jealous isn't much f
either. It's not a happy er
tion. You usually feel jeal
of someone when they ha
something you don't have, l
a new toy. The best way
to feel jealous anymore is
think of all the good things tl
you *do* have.

You might be jealous of y
baby sister. But if you h
take care of her, you'll like
much better. And she'll l
you, too.

FRUSTRATION

When you can't do something you want to do, you feel frustrated. Maybe you're not big enough to climb trees or swim with the older children. You feel frustrated because you can't do the things they do. It's easy to feel frustrated when little things don't work, like zippers and shoelaces. When you feel frustrated you may want to scream or even break what doesn't work.

Your mother tells you to be patient. She says that if you try to make it work again, v-e-r-y slowly, it will be much easier. She's right.

FEAR

Were you ever lost? If you were, you were probably frightened. It's easy to get lost in a supermarket, in the woods, or any place. When you're frightened you have a scary feeling, but it doesn't last long. After you're found it goes away.

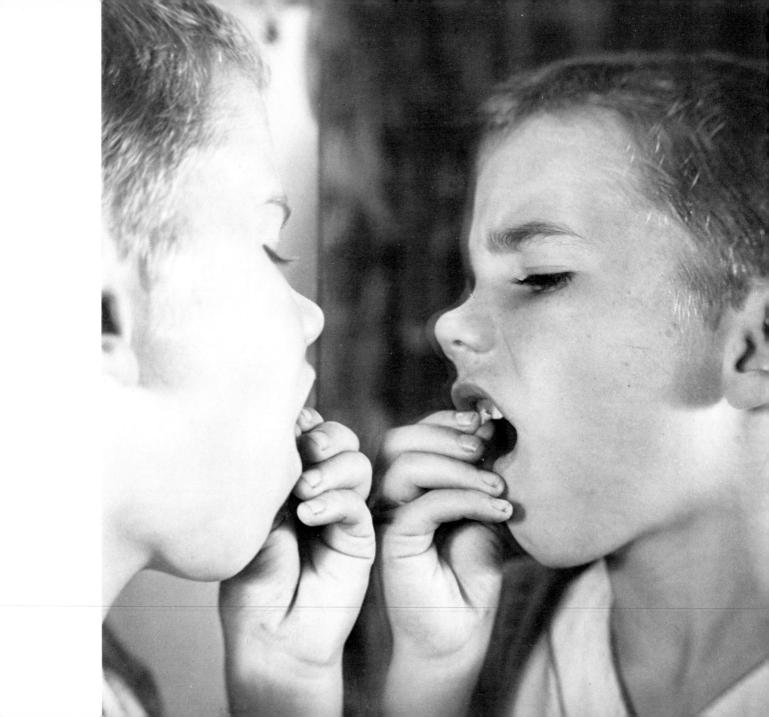

WORRY

Worry is an inside feeling that doesn't always show. You can worry about almost anything: what you've done, what might happen, or how you'll look without a tooth.

The best way to stop worrying
is to tell someone what you're
worrying about. It works.

LONELINESS

Lonely is a very sad way to feel. It's deep inside of you, and stays there until you're not alone any more. It's a quiet kind of sadness. The time you feel the loneliest is when there's no one around. Loneliness goes away when you find a friend to play with.

Sometimes you feel nothing.

SECURITY

Security is a quiet kind of happiness. It's the warm feeling you get when you're with your friends or your family. Security is something you feel way inside of you, like loneliness, but it's happy instead of sad. Maybe it should be called "un-lonely".

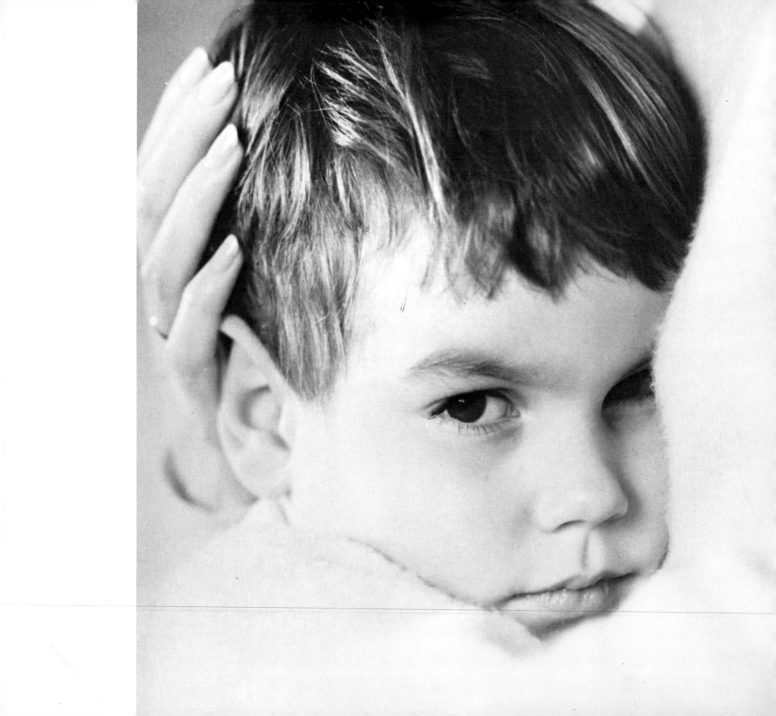

COMFORT

When you hurt yourself and go to your mother, how does she make you feel? You feel better. You feel better when you get close to her. That's what comfort is. Mothers give you a lot of it.

PRIDE

Pride is what you feel when you're pleased with yourself. Inside, you feel happy because you did something just right. Outside, it shows with a big smile. You feel pleased when you make something yourself or when you please someone else. It's nice to feel pleased.

LAUGHTER

What's funny? When someone wears a silly hat or tells a joke, that's funny. When you draw a purple cow, that's funny, too. Clowns are funny. Laughing is funny. Being funny is funny.

JOY

Joy is an all-over feeling, side and out. There isn't ways a reason for joy, you j feel it. You feel it in your h and arms and toes and eve where at once. Sometimes y jump up and down and sh when you feel joy.
There is a special kind of in doing things outdoors.

ABOUT THE AUTHOR AND PHOTOGRAPHERS

The sensitive photographs in this book were taken by an internationally known husband and wife team, Phoebe and Tris Dunn, famous for their pictures of babies, children, young people, family situations and nature subjects. Phoebe Dunn's degree in psychology, says her husband, is largely responsible for the feeling of naturalness and credibility which typifies their work. Results of their busy assignment schedule can be seen regularly on the advertising and editorial pages of major magazines in this country and abroad. As the *Saturday Review* points out, the Dunns are known for their ability to create the kinds of photographs with which readers can easily identify.

Judy Dunn also has a degree in psychology. Her poetry first appeared in print during her undergraduate days at Sweet Briar College and her work has since been published in magazines and poetry periodicals. Following graduation, she was a writer for a large advertising agency in New York. During the past few years, she has written five books about the world of children, all of which reflect her warm understanding of the feelings and activities of youngsters.

It makes you laugh out loud.